black *pearls*

POEMS BY

SHERYL LEIGH ROBERTSON

To black people
To women
Especially black women

With love.

Acknowledgments

I am eternally grateful to God for the gifts He has placed within me: the ability to use words to give shape to thoughts and feelings that many struggle to express, the ability to speak with a conviction and emotion that compels others to listen, and the wisdom to know that even these talents are useless without Him.

To my family—Mom, Dad, Cory, Teresa, David, Tori, Zion, and Roman—thank you for knowing, loving, and encouraging me. To the countless aunts, uncles, and cousins in the Younger, Davis, Robinson, Moorman, and Price families, I appreciate the many opportunities you have given me to share my art in ways big and small. To my grandparents, who are absent from me but present with the Father, I pray that my words bring honor to your names.

I am thankful for every person who has helped me grow in my craft. My True Voices brothers and sisters, you are amazing writers and performers, and you were the iron that sharpened my own. To the event organizers, promoters, churches, and poets who invited me onto stages and platforms that were either thrilling or humbling, thank you; I needed both. To Jasmine Mans, I will always be grateful for your willingness to share your stage with me; in retrospect, it was a moment that solidified my confidence as a spoken word artist. To my Dreamgirls, thank you for providing a safe space for me to dare to imagine all God has for me. To the cohort of black female bloggers who have embraced me and my words, even when I have gone for pitifully long periods of time without sharing either, thank you for inspiring me. To the editors, photographers, and web and graphic designers who have played a part in my messy creative process as well as the finished works of which I am immensely proud, thank you.

To the long list of people I call friend, thank you for reading, listening, and watching. But most importantly, thank you for seeing the person beyond the artist. To everyone who has been a part of my church families, work families, and the social communities to which I belong, thank you for influencing my life experiences, and thus, my art.

Contents

"I recognize that my power as well as my primary oppressions come as a result of my blackness as well as my womanness, and therefore my struggles on both of these fronts are inseparable."
– Audre Lorde

mother of pearl

Mother of Pearl

She wishes nothing
got under her skin.
That words were not swords
slashing so far below the surface
that she is helpless to pinpoint the hurt.
That prejudice
did not penetrate her mind and land in a thud
in her heart.
That cruelty
had never made buffet of her heart,
picking through the bounty of her esteem
and leaving her with scraps.

She wishes nothing got under
her skin.
Yet this is the wonder
of her creation.
That she has power to pull
jewel
from irritant.

That she has built-in balm
for the hurt,
natural protection
from the aggravation.
That if she dare let patience
have its perfect work,[1]
she will build fortress
around every weakness
and nurture it to strength,
she will speak to that which is worthless
and call forth something of value,
she will wrap motherly arms
around unwelcome ugly
and give birth
to unconventional beauty.

She need not pray for thicker skin,
only for peace to endure
the transformation within.

Baptism

Though life experience
has prepared me
for every possible form
of racism and sexism,
each new occurrence
feels like baptism
by fire.

Fifty-Three Percent

When the choice came down
to Trump or Clinton,
the conscience of black women
led them in a direction opposite
most their Caucasian sisters.
According to the numbers
when one's female anatomy comes wrapped in black skin,
she is unable to declare one form of discrimination
more tolerable than the other.

On behalf of the ninety-four percent
for whom cloaking breasts and hips in racial privilege
was not a wardrobe option,
we who did not have the protection
of whiteness
to fall back upon,
we for whom equality is not an issue of political correctness
but a matter of life and death,
we who often face double dose of disrespect
rather than chivalry,
we who feared for our safety
more than for our pocketbooks.
On behalf of those who were not amused
by lewd talk and sexual assault,
excuse us as we wash fresh salt
from ancient gaping wound.

To the forty-three percent
learning that sisterhood takes a backseat to racial allegiance,
we appreciate the sentiment
of marches and clever signage
in support of womanhood.
Yet

When fifty-three percent
of white women voted against women's interests,
a more practical approach
would move the forty-three percent
from the show of city streets
to the intimacy
of kitchen and coffee tables,
sitting across from aunts, cousins, and girlfriends
with whom you do not see eye-to-eye,
asking the uncomfortable question
why.

Family

When women of other races have not embodied the spirit
of sister
When black men have fallen short my understanding
of brother
I am thankful for black women
who have been the unequivocal definition
of family.

"Angry" Black Woman

a better word might be:

frustrated
exasperated
devastated
anguished
tired

aggrieved
unappreciated
overextended
underwhelmed
tired

impassioned
spirited
reserved
disinterested
tired

determined
unconquered
fatigued
exhausted
tired

black hole

Good News

Black mama
come close let me whisper something in your ear:
I know how to get the target off your son's back.

Tell your brown boy to abandon
his uniform white tee
tell him to let go
of his black and grey hoodies
tell him hurry, trade them in
for a black, fur-lined
gorilla suit.[2]

Watch his disguise
slow the hands of the clock when lives are on the line
freeze fingers wrapped anxiously round triggers
challenge minds to consider other options
and weigh down hearts with the gravity
of the decision.

I cannot guarantee an outcome
other than tragedy
but at least
the country will agree
to collective mourning
to speak his name without contempt
to call him a gentle giant.
It will join in when you sing
there's far too many of him dying[3]
pore over studies predicting his extinction
and vow to never let it happen again.

Black mama
help your black boy into a costume of the beast
they have claimed him to be.
Then they will speak of his majesty
they will proclaim his beauty.

The Interrogation

Tell me what you did.
Don't say it was nothing.
You must have done something
to make them hurt you.

Tell me where you were.
And why you were there.
What is it that you said?
Tell me why
you are dead.

Tell me where you have been.
Your upbringing and education.
The company you keep.
Tell me why we should weep
for you.

Prove
Your fate was unfair.
That you are worthy.
Of our outrage, prayers,
the front pages of our publications.
And maybe then
we will call you
a victim.

This is what society says
to the bullet-ridden bodies
of unarmed black people tried
in the court of public opinion.
They are treated as hostile witnesses,
guilty until proven innocent,
and the pettiest of crimes
as capital offenses.

Impartial newspapers remind us:
he was no angel.[4]
The people contend:
if only he'd been more agreeable
or taken care not to resemble
the picture we painted of a criminal
he wouldn't have met this tragic end.

But Jesus
never required someone's perfection
in order to see their pain.
He didn't pass blame
before performing miracles
or laying hands on sick souls.
So where is the Christ in Christians
whose first words to His dying children
are *tell me what you did*?

It's Personal (Black Lives Matter)

This is personal.
Has been since the moment of your arrival
as an ocean of grace
flooded our hearts with joy.
I fell in love with a sweet face overflowing
with cheeks,
stared into big, brown curious eyes
and wondered who you would become:
life of the party or quiet storm?
adventurous explorer or studious book worm?
would you like hoops or baseball?
music or art?
choose Howard or Hampton?
to be a Sigma or Alpha Man?
What is your version
of the American dream?

We do our part:
feed you a steady diet
of love, discipline, and acceptance.
Balance your need for truth
with our desire to protect your innocence.
The only world you've known
is one with Obama as president,
every child your age is a friend,
and you speak of good guys and bad guys
as if there is a clear line of distinction.
You are fascinated with superheroes
and what you consider the human equivalent:
policemen.
They greet you with smiles and high-fives
which you eagerly return and I wish
we could *freeze this frame*—
but we cannot keep you cute and cuddly forever.
Inevitably you will grow
and the rules of engagement will change.

So we stack up dreams for you
like a game of Jenga,
steady hands building unsturdy towers of hope,
praying it doesn't all come tumbling
to the ground.
We've seen it too many times now—
in the pages of our history books,
on the screens of our cell phones and TVs,
on the sidewalks of our communities—
black dreams
outlined in chalk.
Those sights haunt our thoughts
and guide our prayers,
which are as much for your good character
as for the characters who play part in your script.
We know there are many dangers facing you
but we worry most
about those sanctioned by the state
and applauded by the people
in the most blatant displays of hate.
So we pray your protection from concerned citizens
who find the inconvenience of your presence reason
to stand their ground.
We pray that your childhood superheroes
never use their powers for evil,
that your skin does not make you automatic suspect,
that the slightest movement
does not render you a threat.

Because to us
you are a walking miracle,
manifestation of the hope of a prayer circle
that extends backward and forward
through time
until time is no more.
We know that we war
not against flesh and blood

but against principalities and spiritual wickedness.
Yet the casualties
are personal.
Each one represents
a nickname and memories
inside jokes and talents
cheered firsts
and lasts—without ceremony.
Our circle
has prayed, bled, and sacrificed for centuries
with the good faith that someday
its countrymen would not be repulsed
by the assertion that black lives matter,
that this nation with blood-stained hands
would hold a mirror
to its sin,
that black citizens
would have the right
to experience basic human emotions
without them becoming justification
for our deaths,
that this justice system
would not seek to bribe us with millions
when all we ever wanted was a conviction,
that our righteous anger
would not be lumped in
with those who plot vigilante murder,
that society would acknowledge our ability
to mourn officers who are slain
and still refuse to concede
to a system that steals black lives and dreams
while shaming us for our pain.

They say this issue is too controversial.
They expect us to return
to business as usual.
But for us
this is personal.

Black and Blue

I threw the jumbled feelings
from Blue day job and Black 24-hour reality
in a single load into the washing machine of my soul.
On gentle cycle.
An attempt to remove
the sweat rings from the colors' collars
the dark spots from the armpits
the splotches where ripped flesh wept,
without dulling their colors.
With each wash
of the soiled materials,
the stains
slowly began to fade.

But any progress on Black
was undone quickly
sometimes daily,
new splotches mixing with centuries-old blotches
that Blue claimed were produced by Black's own hand.
I kept loading Black back into the washing machine,
laying it out to dry,
reading impractical instructions
for care,
only to see Black repeatedly ripped from clotheslines
and trampled into the dirt.

Until one day
I threw the jumbled feelings
from Blue day job and Black 24-hour reality
in a single load into the washing machine of my soul.
On gentle cycle.
And realized the combined materials
were too soiled
for my heart to manage
without dirtying itself.
That day
I lightened my load
by separating the two.

I folded up Blue day job,
placed it respectfully
back on the pile I naively
pulled it from.
I wondered if it would find its match,
maybe with someone who saw no clash
between Blue and Black,
someone less likely to scrub obsessively
at lingering stains,
a more blended soul
that saw no need for sorting,
that welcomed colors bleeding
one into another.

Missing Names

I don't want to learn another name.
Some mama's baby
nation's maybe,
famed through hashtags
that serve as dog tags
for draftees
of a war
on black bodies.

The first names
I learned without forethought.
Sought the details of their lives and deaths
as if my life
depended on it,
upended society's purported civility,
committed to protest—lest
their deaths
be in vain.

Each name added to the list
became dead weight
piled upon a brain
buckling under the pressure
to maintain an ounce of sanity
and a bleeding heart drained
of viability.
I began to approach new names
with hesitation,
each one a fragile negotiation
between empathy
and self-preservation.

But there is an expiration
date on avoidance.

Names missing from my list
were like a long line of overturned milk cartons,
the spilled contents
pooling in my soul
until they curdled
and reeked
with a hurt that left me gasping for breath.
The refusal to grieve does not postpone
death—
only makes
HEADSTONES
of the living.

To the names missing
from my Black Lives Matter roll call,
I am sorry.
For the times I looked away
as your lifeless body was mauled
by media and the majority.
For the way Iwalkedaroundyourcorpsewithoutpause
on the way to classroom and job
that I knew would not acknowledge you.
For the times I skimmed your name and story,
refused to commit them to memory
in an effort to make home
of this foreign country
that has never welcomed me.

You did not ask
to become another name,
never aspired
to martyr.
Your family likely prayed
this bloody war
would never darken its doorstep,
while we who are left

sidestep
the carnage
as if it is unthinkable
that our homes might be next.

What do a people do when there is no bandage
large enough for the wound?
When ravaged communities are abandoned
by weary souls who can find nothing to salvage?
When the old buggy of faith we rode in on
is well over its mileage
and our collection plate
just shy the mustard seed required for trade-in?
Must we choose
between remembrance
of the fallen
and deference
to depleted souls
that deem missed names
a means of survival?

Fire Escape

Quit fanning the flame.

On the anniversary of Michael Brown's killing,
The Post removed the mystery
of missing names.[5]
It tallied the casualties
of a war that knew neither beginning
nor end, proving
that when police bullets make homes of unarmed bodies,
the victims are disproportionately
black.
Different names
various trespasses
assorted threatening movements—
uniform consequence.

In the infamous Comments section
among the compassion of sympathizers
and declarations of revolutionaries
were foolish notions
made by the willfully ignorant,
reducing hard facts to figments
of dark imaginations,
shifting blame
from perpetrator to truth seeker:
Quit fanning the flame.

As if the fire is fed by anything other
than black bodies.
White supremacy as tinder,
poverty as kindling,
black bones for firewood,
lit with a match of suffering,
breathed on

with the weary sighs of survivors.

When leaping flames died down to embers
this society heaped on
ghettos and gerrymandering,
wage gaps and predatory lending.
This government
claimed spontaneous combustion
while stoking the fire
with raised police batons and slammed jail cells.
The only oxygen fanning flames
is the hot air of post-racial denial
and the stolen breaths
of the missing names.

This blaze that began as bonfire
for your amusement
was fine when it was contained.
But once flames
leapt across MLK Avenues
to threaten downtown revenue,
when protests disrupted your commutes
and disturbed the quiet of your symphonies,
when entire cities
became inferno,
at last
you called for assistance.

But as you stood watch
from a comfortable distance,
water hoses were trained on buildings and bodies alike,
more trauma

inflicted on those who have never known life
without burn,
people who have learned
to function under the constant wail of sirens,
to be lulled to sleep by the rhythm
of snap, crackle, pop,
people who caution their children
to stop, drop, and roll—
though imperfect,
it is more successful than attempts
to raise them to be fire-resistant adults.
These parents cannot prevent
sparks in lives that are flammable
by design.
Generations of bodies and belongings
eaten alive
with no reparations.
Their hearts keep time
to a pendulum swinging
between depression
and hope
that beauty will spring
from this mounting pile of ashes,
that one day Savior
will offer safe passage
through a fire escape of gold.
But today
they strain to breathe
through the smoke's chokehold
on life and dreams,
their smoldering spirits pleading
for rain.

Burn, Baby, Burn

We bust the windows out of cars
with Jazmine,
Keyed four-wheel-drives
with Carrie.
Because a woman scorned has license
to destruct property.

When college students
torched cars and hurled trash cans
as the sports season reached its unsuccessful end
we reasoned:
kids will be kids.

Yet we are angry
when black and brown people act irrationally
after their brothers and sisters are gunned down
and the killers walk free.
The same society that finds compassion
for Jazmines, Carries,

and college students
is at a loss when black lives
are the point of contention.
When tension
has been brewing for centuries longer,
the hurt digs deeper
than the betrayal of a lover,
the stakes higher
than any game.

When it is a matter of black life and death,
why do the rules change?

They do not—
Those who sow injustice
reap calamity.[6]
It is a foolish country
that feigns surprise
when it's finally its turn,
when those it has victimized and marginalized
cry *burn, baby, burn.*

Black Don't Crack

They say *black don't crack.*
But I've seen it
hunched over
like a woman whose kids can't navigate neighborhoods
without stepping on cracks—
or government-backed landmines.
I have seen the kind of brown
with frown lines
etched between eyebrows.
I have discerned nagging worry and dread
penciled across black foreheads.
I have noticed brown eyes framed by dark circles,
a portrait of all the times sleep never came,
the many nights minds tussled
with growing sickness and mounting bills.
I have seen once taut dark skin
sag
like it was pummeled
by life and men,
eyes dead like they internalized the violence.
I have observed tired legs buckling under the load,
as if one more step
might be too much to ask.
I have detected the hurt of heartbreak
spread across once shapely hips
and the slight dips at the corners of mouths
from jaws clenched with family secrets.

I have witnessed
the stress of the many roles tacked onto their identities
nestled in the folds
between the rolls
on black bodies.
Black don't crack
is more than good genes and melanin.
It is also good living,
a few good breaks,
and the absence of the kind of repeated trauma
that drives one to self-medicate.
Black don't crack applies
when life has the decency
to offer periods of kindness
to break up the blocks of distress.

So when I glance at my reflection
I am thankful for the life and chances
I have been given.
I am grateful for the times I have desperately reached up
and managed to touch heaven.
Because I can see all around me
that even black skin can eventually tell
how close it has come
to hell.

Must Love Dogs

If America created an online dating profile
it would read:
Two hundred thirty-nine year old white male
seeks meek
young, healthy, and moderately wealthy
conservative Christian.
Preferably Caucasian
but open to variations of light skin from any regions
other than Africa and the Middle East.
And last but certainly not least
must love dogs.

Must respect the sacredness
of the bond between man and his best friend.
After all
from bouncy pup to slow-gaited old timer
a dog is loyal to the end.
A cozy furball to snuggle up to in all of life's seasons
a companion that never outgrows its need for you
a breed you can train to blindly obey:
eat! lay! sit! stay!
The kind of love you can put on a leash.

A dog is easy to love—
but people
are wild and free
with minds that cannot be controlled
moods that change without notice
behavior that is hard to respect
mouths prone to barking politically incorrect foolishness.
Human beings are hard to love.
So all dogs go to heaven
but a person

can be sentenced to the darkest pits of hell
for a mistake.
We have no problem stooping over
to scoop up the feces left behind by canines
but run
from the messes that humans make—
even if their only crime is in being poor.
I long for the Northwest DC of 15 years ago,
a sea of black faces.
But now the sidewalks are swimming
with yuppies and puppies,
Rockies and Fidos curled up beside tables
as their masters dine on restaurant patios
that natives cannot afford.
Meanwhile
I hear stories of noise complaints
for kids bouncing balls on pavement,
of adjustments to homecoming traditions
to reduce the crowds and keep down the music,
teaching black children two lessons:
to be apologetic for taking up space
and that they can be pushed aside when others realize
they've been sleeping on prime real estate.
I've begun to notice a trend
in which communities carve out spots
where we can see Spot run.
But for all the dog parks popping up
I wonder are there enough playgrounds for children
affordable houses to live in
grocery stores and community gardens
to quench the thirst of food deserts.

For where your treasure is
there your heart will be also.
How can we claim to love our neighbors

whom we treat like strangers
while making dogs a part of the family?
How can people go to bat for animals with such ferocity
yet remain silent
on the atrocities perpetrated against human beings?
How could the sight of dog-fighting ring master Michael Vick
in a Steelers jersey after prison
cause more outrage than a quarterback
who has twice faced rape allegations
and players who beat women and children?
I would argue
that the same officials who declared Flint's water suitable
would sing a different tune
if that cloudy, lead-laced liquid
appeared in their own puppies' water bowls.
And if ever there were a pattern
of dogs being gunned down
a chant of *dogs' lives matter!*
would not produce as much anger
as proclaiming that black ones do.

America
can create a beautiful dating profile—
picture-perfect with a gleaming smile
and the words *What Would Jesus Do?*
listed among its favorite quotations.
But the wise will call catfish
when they realize the hypocrisy
at the heart of this one nation
under God
for whom loving dogs is mandatory
while it is optional
to love me.

In Search of Home

Ripped
from villages.
Unsettled
on plantations.
Stiffed
forty acres.
Shackled to
sharecropped land.
Boxed in
by red lines.
Sequestered
in ghettoes.
Stuck in
riots' ruins.
Turned away from
doors locked by foreclosure.
Packing up
with notice of eviction.
Pushed out
by gentrification.
Running from
tenant blacklists.
Most African Americans
have always been in search
of home.

Those who find it
hold on for dear life
to this place where they will raise children,
to this piece of earth to which generations
can return
no matter how far life carries them,
to this haven where love is spoken fluently,
to this sacred space overflowing
with blood equity.

Something in the Water

There's something in the water.
Of the Atlantic:
Unrecognizable bodies
loved in distant lives,
nameless in death.
Obstinate chains and defiant bones
sunken to depths
unknown
and scattered across ocean floor.
That something in the water
is an eternal echo of the screams
of the innocent,
the vestiges
of stolen dreams.

There's something in the water.
Of the Bayou:
The bloated bodies
of those perpetually stranded
by circumstance and finance.
The tattered doilies
that once had a place at every family dinner.
The blurred passages of diaries
that held more family history than mouths will ever utter.
That something in the water
is the cherished fragments of modest lives,
the despair of drowning dreams,
memories gasping for air.

There's something in the water.
Of Flint:
Specks of greed,
traces of neglect,
the ink of discarded memos
flowing to the taps of unsuspecting homes.
A truth more repugnant
than the liquid's odor.
That something in the water
is a fraudulent definition
of clean,
a contamination
of devalued dreams.

For black folks
there has always been something in the water.
That uproots and carries away.
That turns natives into castaways.
That makes wreckage of prized possessions.
That muddies vision
and suffocates ambition.
That infiltrates happiness
and soaks up hope.

But it is man's evil
that reveals ugliness in what God called beautiful.
There is something greater in the water
than the power that destroys.
There is a presence
that buoys up
those swept into currents.

That sustains rather than smothers.
That heals instead of inflicting pain.
That offers refuge from bloodhounds.
That engulfs the confounded
in peace.
That cleanses of sin
and the fingerprints of vile men.
That baptizes and restores souls
to God's original plan.
The water is proof
that good and evil must coexist —
but the light shines in the darkness
and the darkness can never extinguish it.[7]
There is indeed
something in the water.
Both in calm and in conflict,
it will never be absent
the Father.

Prison Break

Master and Warden
Judge and Congressman
Put too much confidence
In shackles
Invisible fences
And solitary confinement.
They were too arrogant
With claims of emancipation
And reconstruction,
Civil rights
And justice,
Too reckless
With language
Like slave
Inmate
Nigger
Law and order
Productive citizen.

Powerful and debilitating
As centuries of schemes may be,
Uprising
Is imminent,
Prison breaks
An inevitable aspect of advent,
A requirement
Of a people who decline to define
Themselves
As anything other
Than prisoners
Of hope.

It Ain't Over

I wonder if our ancestors thought it was over.
Hauled over endless miles of ocean,
location: unknown.
Bodies packed in like cattle,
minds saddled
with the darkness of a present reality
against the backdrop
of bright memories.
Trying to discern between a silent God
and an absent one.
Destination: unknown.

I wonder if their survival
convinced those who came after them
of God's presence.
A generation up from slavery
but still bowed over
land that did not belong to them
and water fountains designated for them,
following orders dictated to them,
relegated to second-class citizenry
in the land of the free.
Brutalized and dehumanized
yet with eyes on the prize,
minds stayed on Jesus.

I wonder if these examples of inexplicable survival
remind a new generation
stuck

between the manifestation of a dream
and the threat of its reversal
that the struggle
ain't over.

With the prevalence of senseless violence
in communities of people who look like us,
with the relevance
of diversity and affirmative action called into question,
with the Voting Rights Act on the chopping block,
we might feel like we got the breath knocked
right out of us.

But it ain't over.
Because of the remarkable stories
of a long line of people destined
to overcome.
Today
somewhere between the echoes of ringing freedom
and the roar of protest,
we are hard pressed on every side
yet not crushed,
perplexed
but not in despair.[8]
Life for us ain't been no crystal stair[9]
but all the while we've been climbing.

Our story is as much triumph as it is tragedy.
We are warriors —

of the Buffalo Soldier and Tuskegee Airmen variety.
We are the gifted hands
that handed the world hieroglyphics
and performed the first open-heart surgery,
the brilliant minds
that organized the nation's first blood banks.
We are owed a debt of thanks
for carrying jazz and blues in our womb,
for giving birth to soul and hip hop,
for unearthing lucrative cash crops in a land
whose soul was enslaved to cotton.
Like Cotton Club phenom Josephine Baker and Alvin Ailey,
we are dance.

We are heavyweights—physical and lyrical—
from Muhammad Ali to Lauryn Hill.
We are justice,
Eric Holder standing on the shoulders
of Thurgood Marshall.
We are the wives married to the struggle
as much as to the man—Coretta, Betty, and Winnie.
We are the writers of stories
no one else dared tell—
Ida B. Wells and Billie Holiday
calling out the blood on the leaves of southern trees
and Robert Johnson giving us pages upon pages of black
as beautiful.

We are artful athleticism
from Jesse Owens to Venus and Serena.
We are humanitarianism
from Belafonte to Mandela.
We are renaissance and revolution
Harlem and Ferguson.
We are the ones they didn't guess were coming to dinner—

Fannie Lou Hamer in the registrar's office
the Little Rock Nine climbing the steps of Central High
and the Obamas taking up residence in the White House.
We are the embodiment of for us, by us
from HU to Morehouse
and Black Wall Street to Madam CJ's beauty line.

Because our bloodline
produced kings long before Martin.
We were queens of Sheba and Cleopatra fame
well before Latifah reigned.
And if not in the physical,
we can all be spiritual descendants of royalty.
Sons and daughters of the most high King.
Living in this moment between salvation and glory
no longer who we were
but it does not yet appear what we shall be.[10]

So we are grateful
as we look back and wonder how we made it over.
Yet we are still prayerful
ever hopeful
that while the struggle may not be over
we still have the will
to overcome.

blackboard

Michelle and Maxine

Michelle
Girl of the South Side
Who from campaign trail to White House
Withheld side eye
From those most deserving.
Who walked the line between speaking your truth
And not needlessly offending.
Who showed us
Sometimes standing by your man
Means moments of silence in the presence of critics
To ensure his success.
Michelle
Who did not plaster fake smiles on your face
For the sake of a prejudiced partisan press.
Who demonstrated that wise compromise
Does not make one any less
Strong black woman.
Michelle
Who withstood microscopic lens
For the greater good
Of family, country, race, and womanhood,
Thank you.
You are grace personified,
Source of pride for women and girls worldwide,
But especially
Those who are black and blessed
To have seen you as FLOTUS
And still one of us.

Maxine
Veteran politician
With the audacity to say just what you mean.
Strong black woman
Who has walked this path too many times
To be intimidated or undermined.
Seasoned saint

With the level of boldness that comes
When the only thing on the line
Is freedom.
Maxine
Who after decades of service
Has earned every right to rest on your laurels,
But unsatisfied with yesterday's progress,
Continues the fight with passion, conviction
And the occasional well-timed eye-roll.
Who cannot be bothered to compose a poker face
Because all your cards are on the table
Face up.
Thank you
For your willingness to articulate
That which position or circumstance does not permit us to say.
Thank you for being an assertive voice of opposition
In a world that raises girls to be women
Who go along to get along
And sacrifice being right
In the interest of being liked.
We live vicariously through your moxie,
Reassured by grandmas and mamas
That we will inherit it
With maturity.

Michelle and Maxine,
Whose words and appearance have gone viral
With both praise and disapproval,
We see ourselves
In you.
We needed the example
Of each of you.
So thank you
For showing us and the world
That there is more than one way
To be a strong black woman
And that the version we choose
Must fit our purpose and our season.

Us and Them

Dear black folk,
you've been known to devote
entire lifetimes and generations
to proving Chris Rock's assertion
that there is an *us* and a *them*:
black people and niggas.
Oh the hoops you jump through
the heights you climb to
the magic tricks you enact
the mental stunts you perform.
All to ensure you meet societal norms,
all to assure doubtful citizens
you are different than
better than
the niggas.

But in the brief moments before
names are exchanged
when you are without the company
of your framed degrees
when you are not shielded
by occupation
pedigree
political affiliation —
in those seconds before you can explain
just how remarkable you are
all of our black
looks the same.

Dear them that is us,
you don't have to be exceptional
to be beautiful.
You don't have to dot every I
or cross every T
for your story to be worth the read.
You don't have to hold each inch
of your life against a ruler
of socially accepted increments
trying to measure
up.
You can be regular
and still matter.
You can be imperfect
and deserving of respect.

Dear us that is them,
no matter what
you do or don't do
no matter who
you are or are not,
by virtue
of your humanity
you are enough.

Boot Straps

Some folks pull themselves up
by their own boot straps,
step away from their humble beginnings
and fall into the trap
of demanding others do the same,
forgetting
their straps were wrapped
with the strength of extraordinary talent and wit,
reinforced
with the sturdy leather of tough love,
handed down
a few sizes too large,
leaving room to grow into them.
Those folks don't speak
of the hands
that placed the boots on their feet,
seasoned meals with love,
gave proud pats on the back,
slapped egos upside their too-big heads,
ran warm tubs of water to soak blistered feet,
used needle and thread to repair tears in the fabric,
and folded routinely in prayer
asking God
to bless the journey.

Silly of this village, expecting
those who pulled themselves up by their boot straps
to graciously extend a hand
back.

"Black-on-Black Crime"

If the world's first murder
was brother-on-brother,
is it any wonder
in a country that packs
black men into city centers
with nothing but blocks and corners
to call their own,
that fragile, power-hungry egos shatter
upon impartial pavement,
the fragments
clumsily pieced back together
by Cains unrepentant
for the deaths of Abels?
That pristine Js step over pools
of blood boiling
with the anger
of brothers with no keepers?

"Black-on-black crime"
is too heavy a burden for even
an entire race's shoulders.
No sin
has befallen the black man
but such as is common to man.

Colorblind

How apropos
of America
to proudly diagnose
itself
colorblind.

For its citizens with mild cases,
the nation's subtle beauties
go unseen.
Their eyes spy
nothing but green
in the blades
of Kentucky's bluegrass,
Georgia's red clay
is merely a mound
of brown,
and the heartland's
plains of amber grain
a lackluster beige.

But for the countrymen
whose colorblindness is most severe,
for those whose sensitive eyes shy
away from the light,
Black and White
are their color spectrum's
dominant shades,
labeling everything in between
an inconsequential gray.

Old Glory

What to the slave[11]
is the Star-Spangled Banner?
His **red** blood
baked into American soil like a secret ingredient
for national success.
Her back bent over rows of **white** cotton,
empty hands gathering another's harvest.
Blue uniforms standing on front lines
and behind chow lines
in the fight for freedom.

What to the newly emancipated
is Old Glory?
A **Red** Record of lynching's horror.
White hoods turning a cross of redemption
into a symbol of terror.
Melancholy melodies
making artform of a people's **blues**.

What to the colored person
is the Stars and Stripes?
The **Red** Summer white mobs bludgeoned black bodies
from sea to shining sea.
White coats making guinea pig of black patients.
Bodies of **blue** water crossed by native sons searching the globe
for acceptance.

What to the Negro
is the Red, White, and Blue?
Red-lined neighborhoods drawing his children out
of the American dream.
Bernice's **white** hair bows against Coretta's chest
as her dreamer father took his rest.
A **blue** marquee marking a corner where hate exploded,
Burying faith and little girls in the rubble.

What to the black person
is the American flag?
The **red** bulb of Walter Scott's dead brake light.
The **white** car that was backdrop for Rodney King's pummeling
The **Blue** Wall of Silence,
impenetrable even by videotaped evidence.
To African-American millennials
who know the gloom of the grave[12] has been inescapable
throughout their people's history,
the American flag becomes a symbol
of deep-seated hypocrisy
and its anthem
a reason to remain seated.

Open Arms

Too tactful to chisel
her true feelings into the base of a statue,
when America placed Lady Liberty
as beacon along her shores,
she used a sonnet
written by a descendant of immigrants
to present an image to the world:

Give me your tired, your poor,
your huddled masses yearning to breathe free.[13]

But the fine print
engraved on her heart
belied the warm welcome sign:

Give me your Zumba and salsa,
teach my feet to flow to the rhythm of your soca,
my hips to shimmy with your belly dances.
Pile my plate with your curry and empanadas,
fill my cup with your coffee and tequila.
Hang your intricate masks on my walls,
place your delicate ceramics on my table.
Clothe me in scarves made with your vibrant textiles,
adorn my wrists with your beads and jewels.
Give me your cornrows, braids,
the very hair on your head
for my wigs and weaves.
Tell me your fables and folklore,
read me your proverbs and poetry —
so I may call myself cultured.

I have no desire

to learn the history of the culture
that brought you here.
I will love your outer eccentricity
but ignore the humanity
within.
I will claim to understand your brethren
based on my limited interaction with a few.
If one of you dare sin
in the same ways I've seen countless citizens,
I will claim it is all of you.
In one breath I will say I love diversity,
and in the next I will ask,
"Why can't you be more like me?"

King Reimagined

The irony
that Martin Luther King, Jr. boulevards
are sites of the same poverty and blight,
housing inequality and police brutality,
injustice and violence
that their namesake spoke against.
Street signs are pageantry
when the surrounding communities
cash checks of promised opportunity
only to be told
the funds in America's moral bank account
are still insufficient.

The selective memory
of those who invoke his name
to condemn protest.
Those who forget
today's national hero
was yesterday's uppity negro,
traitor,
agitator of the status quo.
Those who commemorate his birthdate
with excerpts of "I Have a Dream"
but never "Why We Can't Wait."

The denial
of those who view him as second messiah
come to save America of her sins.
The spilled blood of one of God's chosen
never carried the weight
of that of His only begotten Son,
will never be capable
of making restitution
for wrong committed against a people.

I imagine King

looks down from mountaintop
standing beside the King of Kings —
one who has seen
His own life and purpose reimagined
and says:
I wish they would leave my name out of it.

Woke

Team No Sleep
must not know
that "woke"
"sleep walking"
and "dead to the world"
are not the only categories of black
existence.
During times that try men's souls,[14]
common sense
says the articulation of pain
must be balanced
with submission
to rest.
It is the only way to win
the enduring fight
of revolution.

A Guarded Heart

A heart known to flinch
from paper cuts
and hemorrhage
after trauma
is impossible to protect.
Rather than construct
impenetrable walls around its tenderness
or lock its prized benevolence
behind metal gates,
I have simply learned to pray:
Lord, help me
not to hate.

casting pearls before swine

Who Will Fight for Girls?

When grown men's appetite for adolescence
plays out with militants
snatching children from boarding school dorm rooms,
who will fight for girls?
Gunmen on the lookout
as a convoy steals away with 276 units
of precious cargo.
Six hundred days later,
their families still don't know their whereabouts.
Rumors of forced marriages and sexual slavery
fly with lightning speed, but time
marches slowly, heavy
with the burden of missed sweet sixteens
and the silence of a world that has forgotten.
We snidely ask how Nigeria could let such a thing happen
but there are children in America suffering the same fate
hidden in plain sight.
Here teenage girls slip away one by one,
easy prey
for opportunists who sniff out their need for attention.
And it is hard to muster public sympathy
for this modern-day slavery
when we insist on calling it prostitution.
They are still children
not old enough to consent,
yet bought and sold
across interstates and Internet
as the trail grows cold.

Who will fight for girls
when the choice is between her body
and his reputation,
when the story is always framed as
womanly wiles destroying a good man?

As society debates not just whether Cosby did it
but the innocence of dozens of women involved,
it is no coincidence that many believers
also paint a curious picture
of King David's sin.
How quickly some jump to the conclusion
that Bathsheba must have been immodest—
when for all we know
she could have been minding her business,
bathing in a suitable location,
when David strolled his palatial rooftop
and caught a glimpse.
How naively some suggest *she* should have refused
in order to prevent *his* sin.
Needless speculation
when the Bible is clear on one thing:
God's displeasure
with David's abuse of power.
So who fights for girls
when the church is not a safe haven,
when our exegesis
finds female manipulation and temptation
even when it doesn't exist,
constantly putting womanhood at odds with salvation?

Who will fight for girls when misogynists
are as blatant and clueless
as racists?
Woman is both punching bag
and punchline.
Either dimepiece
or worthless.
Always *too emotional*,
her legitimate anger chided
as bitterness.

When lyrics

paint her as the enemy,
but artists call her lover
once the song fades out.
When she is edited straight outta
biopics and biographies
despite being integral to the story.
When telling the gory details of her own
is deemed *bringing the black man down*
though, throughout history,
no one has ever been more down for black men
than black women.

So who will fight for black girls?
When they are Sandra Bland,
society arguing whether her death was by her own hands
when regardless
persons and systems were complicit.
When she is expected to produce cheer and smile
on demand.
When people pick fights with her
then cry foul
when she defends herself the only way she knows how:
with words.
What she says may not be nice or pretty
but she believes it her only ammunition
in a fight that was never fair.
Who will defend her
when she has been manhandled
and her dignity trampled?
When darkness sets
night after night
in a lonely, windowless cell
and she loses sight of the light of the God within?
When hope is swallowed up by the walls
and the fight abandons her soul?
Because yes, black girls may be magic
but they tire of being invisible.
And perhaps their greatest trick

is convincing the world they are invincible,
when beneath the glitter,
they are still flesh and bone
and deep down in the soul
of every strong black woman
lives a vulnerable little girl
who wishes someone
would fight for her.

And I think deep down in every man
is the person God has called him to be:
partner and protector
of God's daughters.
But when men's chests are swollen
with so much pride that their hearts become infected
and the question
who will fight for girls?
continues to go unanswered,
I am forever beholden
to One whose ego
was not too fragile to handle
two sisters asking where He had been.
One whose heart
made room for both virgins
and women who'd known five husbands.
One whose wisdom knew
that freeing a woman of her demons
breeds the kind of loyalty that outlasts Calvary.
One whose divinity
viewed them as persons long before it saw them as women.
One who knows how it feels to be desired
but not loved.
That gracious man from Galilee,
whose response to the question
who will fight for girls?
has always been:
Lord, send me.

Rhythm and Blues *(a coming of age)*

They ask me if I feel different now.
Does this heart beat
more quickly, rapid staccato taps
on snare drum?
Does my body twist
wild and playful
to the rhythm,
head bobbing
lanky arms and legs snapping
movements choppy
jerky,
too naive to be self-conscious
of what it is becoming?
Or is my heartbeat
the heavy
steady pounding
on a bass,
sultry blues and yearning soul,
effortless sway and seduction,
the fluid rolling
of womanly curves in slow motion?

They ask me if I feel different now.
How can I explain
that there are two sides to this drum?
I am both snare and bass,
a two-faced
being
in a world that demands
I choose.

I am a girl clinging
to innocence,
body flung
into womanhood.

They look at me as if
I am different now.
They expect me
to bow in curtsy
like a lady.
So I tuck in
the girl who has yet to comprehend
the finality
of goodbye,
tell her this is the deal
we involuntarily cut
with nature,
remind her
big girls don't cry
and promise what I cannot deliver—
that some day
I'll come back for her.

Missing

When the faces of the missing
don't resemble the all-American girl—
are less Natalee Holloway
and more around-the-way girl,
are less Ivy Park
and more trailer park—
when they dare
come from troubled backgrounds
or hang with questionable crowds...

There are no search teams assembled
to reclaim their parents' stolen dreams,
no news stations flashing smiling portraits
across TV screens,
no advocates to question a public conscience
that transforms "fast" girls into consenting women
able to mentally and physically spar
with grown men.

At best
there is a flurry
of family and community activity—
calls, texts, e-mails, social media postings
that cannot begin to tell the intricacies
of these girls' stories.
While it is a rally
to inform the world,
it is more importantly
a message to girls
both lost and present:
though others may not notice your absence,
you are missed
valued
loved
here
as our girls.

Blushing Brides

When father
is always
guardian of virtue
and watchman of virginity
but never
impenetrable wall
shielding fragile heart,
when his perception of protection
prioritizes economic security
over emotional safety,
underage daughters
are shepherded to altars
like lambs to the slaughter.

For some,
their innocence cloaked in ornate clothing
and crowned with elaborate jewels,
it is a game of dress-up
before family and friends.
But others know this is not pretend.
Fear unveiled,
feet moving at snail's..........................
pace,
hands trembling,
wide-eyed
blushing brides.

Yet the naive are also right.
It is a game of make-believe,
a parade

of girls forced to play women.
Childhoods cast aside
in moments
as they learn a lifelong lesson:
to be woman
is to be possession
legal tender
changing hands without a say;
womanhood is a lifelong debt
that can never be paid;
to be woman
is to have body
soul
dreams
perpetually bartered away.

Vulnerable

Women are chastised
for building walls
indestructible.
They are told
independence must not overshadow
their ability to be vulnerable.

There is little acknowledgment
that emotional walls
do little
to protect the physical.
There is little recognition
of a painful reality:
there is a vulnerability in womanhood
that is involuntary.

Twenty Minutes

A society that lectures daughters
to respect themselves
but does not bother
to admonish sons
to respect everyone as themselves
is demonstrated in fathers
who pen letters
defending men who have assaulted,
without mention
of the women violated.
Fathers who legitimize
as *action*[15]
that for which she was not active
participant.
Fathers who do not characterize
as violent
invasion of a woman's body.
Fathers who summarize
as *20 minutes*
what for her
is recurring nightmare.
Fathers who plead
for their convicted sons' dreams
without concern
for the assaulted women's welfare,
rationing regard like welfare—
begrudgingly,
assigning shame to basic necessity.

A society that produces parents
who lecture the wrong party
and misdirect sympathy
is destined to create judges
who agree.

Conduct Unbecoming

Any woman unfortunate
to become victim
of a man's wrath or lust
must hope no one digs
far enough
in her past
to reveal any conduct unbecoming
a lady.
Or the response will surely be
she had it coming.

Just Say No

I don't know when my life's purpose
was reduced
to putting other people at ease.
Don't know how I assumed responsibility
for everyone's contentment.
Don't know why it has become second nature
to place my well-being second
to others' comfort.

All I know
is I am a grown woman who tiptoes
down city streets as if the pavement
were lined with egg shells.
Despite racing mind and introverted temperament,
I pause long enough to greet strange men
who deem me the momentary object
of their attention.
How casually I extend the olive branch of hello
to prevent arguments
of whether I think myself *too cute*.
When did I become astute
in words and movements
that uphold fragile male egos?
When did the muscles of my mouth learn to morph
into something between a grimace
and a grin
at the risk
of being called *too pretty to look so mean*?
When did I become machine
responding to others' commands as if I were created
for their ease?

I have spent my whole life
being polite.
Mastered nice
before I conquered long division,
never solving how many times one could divide self
before diminished
into increments
indistinguishable.
Regrettably
I offer my *no* coated with niceties
and lavished with apology
because I do not want to argue,
because unwanted flirtation is less taxing
than confrontation.
Admittedly
I do it because I am afraid
of becoming the next victim
of male pride.
Read stories of weapons
exacting bloody revenge on women
who complained of hands on their backsides,
who declined a little bump and grind,
who chose not to give him the phone number—
reminders that chance encounters
can turn deadly
when a woman dares deny access
to her space or body.

I am guilty
of feeding the beast of male entitlement
lest it eat me alive.
It is easier to call my cordial
response to strange men
a means of survival
rather than admit
I have no control.

When I read stories of these murdered women
I cannot name a single thing
I would have done differently.
Then I become angry
with myself
For picking apart their actions and attitudes
in search of mistakes,
as if they had responsibility
to a man's feelings
while he invaded their personal space,
as if grace
is still expected
even as a woman is being accosted.
Even "nice" does not protect
against men who never learned to accept
rejection.
Safety is but an illusion
for women who stroll city streets as if the pavement
were lined with booby traps.
Despite your attempts
to sidestep danger,
you never know when an entitled man
will snap.

Hero

When faced with a mugger,
Women are told:
Don't be a hero.
Do not fight back.
Let the purse and money go.
Nothing is worth more
Than your life.

Yet when the thief comes
For her body,
She is expected
To claw faces
And dig nails into wrists
As evidence
She was forced.

When a part of her being
Becomes the stolen goods,
Perhaps fighting does not always look
Like kicks, scratches, bites, and blows.
In agonizing moments of personal invasion
In which every part of her wants to die,
The greatest act of courage and resistance
Is to survive.

black *pearls*

Black Pearls

How many times has the world been turned
upside down
in the name of the diamond?
How often have men
dug up rich earth
and mined fruitful ground
in search of her shine?
How many souls have been sold
for a chance encounter
with the diamond's glitter?
Seduced by her sparkle,
how many heads have bowed at Earth's altar
begging for a gleaming miracle?
How much blood dots the leaves
and courses through streams
of regions and countries
that sought diamond
as source of power and salvation?
How much propaganda has been spun
to present her as the standard of beauty,
how many adjustments made
to manipulate her rarity,
how many lies told
to authenticate her purity?
At whose expense
did the industry calculate her expense?

What of the other gems—
overlooked
unappreciated
disregarded
made to feel less than?
What of the precious stones
regarded as rhinestone
simply because they are not diamond?
Far from counterfeit,

these originals
are equally beautiful
no less valuable—
yet not chosen,
lacking the publicity and promotion needed
to elicit global affection.

What of the other gems?
What becomes
of the little-known black pearl?
Does she beg the world
to take notice of her elegance?
Does she hope it will look past the diamond's flash
to see her substance?
In the past
she would emerge from the diamond's shadow,
twisting and turning in the sunlight,
and wonder why people were not enchanted
by her iridescent glow.
Then she realized
just as rainbows
go unappreciated by the colorblind,
some cannot look past conditioned minds
to truly see her.

Yet she does not require their gaze
to stand in the truth of her glory.
She is exquisite
precious
treasured collaboration
between God and nature
a portrait
of exceptional strength.
Man may manufacture markets
in which diamonds are the prized jewel
but God appraised her invaluable
the moment He made her
black pearl.

Origami

A woman learns to fold
inwardly
inventively
like origami,
finished product
whatever you need her to be.

She thinks this trick
makes her more interesting
more likeable.
She is relieved when the crowd marvels
at the many shapes made of her.
But she can't tell
whether she is admired
for her creativity
or exploited
for her flexibility.

She claims her contortions
harmless.
She rationalizes
changes made without scissors
can be undone.
But in time,
simple folds leave permanent creases.
With each new shape
she veers further from the original.
Unable to smooth out the crinkles,
incapable of making
the bends less noticeable,
she folds herself
again and again
until there is nothing left
but the flimsy, ragged
remains
of what she used to be.

Intervention *(for Lil' Kim)*

Where were you before?
You who prefer her brown-skinned
with the heart-shaped face of Hard Core.
You who miss the lips of Notorious
the wide nose and sharp cheekbones
of the one who claimed rap's throne
as Queen Bee.
You who are so vocally partial to the original
Lil' Kim,
where were your words of affirmation
when she was still brown girl
in a world that reserved royalty for whiteness
in a community taught to place lightness
on a pedestal
in an industry that made fetish
of mixed chicks?
Where were your compliments for dark pigment
when she needed them?

Was it the braggadocios bars
that fooled you?
Among the talk of wealth, houses
talent and sexual prowess
did you not notice
her boasting referenced body but not face?
Could you not detect the pretense
in her calculated confidence?
Did the clever wordplay effectively downplay
her inadequacy?
Did you forget that sexy
is not synonymous with pretty?
Did you consider
long before she settled for sex symbol
she was a girl whose sole desire
was to be beautiful?
Did you not think it cut her

when the love of her life took her to bed
and a light-skinned church girl to the altar?
Did you think her too *bad bitch* to bleed?
Did you assume Queen Bee
was less woman, less human
because she never patched her heart to her sleeve?
Did you not see it happening
one nip one tuck at a time
a gradual lightening?
A little correction here
little enhancement there
a continuous fading
from black
to white caricature.
If you could backtrack a few decades
to the first time she played artist with her features,
if you could pick up on the clues of each nip,
would you spare her the guilt trip
of your current judgement
by telling her the moment she steps on the scene
that her black is beautiful?

Even then
perhaps you would already be too late,
groundwork already laid
by father, boyfriends, boys on the block.
Maybe little Kimberly Jones learned
in the school of hard knocks
that she was never quite pretty enough,
that *regular black girl*[16]
just ain't good enough.
Maybe fame's spotlight highlights
all the things about yourself
you've ever wanted to change.
Charge it to the game
that fattens pockets and tempts humans
to take life and anatomy
into their own hands.

The only difference between our Kim
and their Kardashian
is one had a head start,
less melanin and ethnicity to overcome
in pursuit of her view of perfection.
And all that separates Lil' Kim
from countless dark women on every continent
who make lightening cream a part of their daily regimen
is access to the money to make the change drastic
and permanent.
Maybe they were all once little girls
with star-crossed eyes trained on an image
of gorgeous,
staring into mirrors
calculating the change needed as down payment
on beautiful,
paying attention
to the world's response to women
and noting the deficit
of those with more pigment,
deciding that ladies with light skin, long hair,
hourglass figures and European features
had a monopoly on pretty,
that the world never played fair
because dark women rarely got a chance
and when they did
their turns were always cut short by waterworks
from broken hearts.

It is too late to return to start
and affirm Lil' Kim and women like her.
Yet there are impressionable girls
watching
listening
waiting
for acknowledgment and shameless endorsement
of their brand of beautiful.

Round of Applause

Search
every inch of your being.
Locate
the part that aches
for social media "likes."
Find
the piece of you obsessed
with page views.
Pinpoint
the perfectionist who feels inadequate
without a standing ovation.
Heap upon her
the affirmation
she seeks from others.
Drape your arms
across her drooped shoulders,
tell her
not to put much stock in the recognition
of men.
Explain
her value does not fluctuate
according to their attention.
Assure her
she is as worthy on her worst day
as on her best,
that she exists
for a purpose greater
than applause.
Her life is not a performance,
but participatory art
with an audience
of One.

Timid

Never tiptoe
across the deep sea of your soul
trying not to make waves
with people not brave enough
to dip toe
let alone wade
beyond your shores.

For Harmony's Sake

I sacrificed my voice
for the sake of harmony.
Yet there are parts
when the composer intended someone
to carry the melody.

Thirty-Something

I have been humbled
at thirty-something
to find myself facing
every issue of the heart
my twenty-something-self pushed aside
rather than conquer.
I have learned
progress is not permanent,
some demons must be cast out again
and again,
and you only grow to the extent
you're willing to revisit
places you have already been.

There are lessons back there.
Wisdom buried
at the bottom of boxes you hastily packed as you fled
without warning,
etched on the face of the person
with whom it pains you to make eye contact,
written in the script of scenes you impulsively reenact...
and later regret,
inscribed in fiction
you mistook for fact,
hitched to dreams stolen
when you were too timid to fight back.

At thirty-something
I have caved to a wanderlust soul
mastering time-travel
between present-day angst and the lessons
back there.

I am still learning to find meaning
in being my own.

to shun the private shame
of not being someone else's,
to not seek salvation
in a changed last name.
I am still accepting singleness
is not punishment
for sins long forgiven
or the disadvantage
of being damaged
goods.
I am still fighting to reject suggestions
that I am difficult to love,
too much complexity and sensitivity,
too little dependence and openness,
anything other than just right
for the right one.
I am still conceiving
a grace-induced evolution
to just-right status
that accounts for my imperfections.
I am still struggling
not to carry the hurt of lost loves
like untreated battle wounds,
turning relationships into emergency rooms
and placing bleeding heart in the hands of men
not qualified to operate.
I am still discovering
that healing comes during the wait,
in the hushing of voices
that tell me I have been forgotten,
that say my house is silent,
that claim my bed is empty,
as if my presence

does not count for anything,
as if there is no value
in my voice,
as if I am not a full person on my own—
ample mind, body, and spirit
to fill a home.

I am realizing
both the challenge and beauty
of thirty-something
is no different than
the joy and heartache
of any age.
It is always
the learning.

Home

God bless the child
who has come into her own.
The one who takes up residence
in an unconventional body
without seeking permission
or offering apology.
She whose face is soaked in melanin,
whose vast dimensions
scoff at measuring tape,
whose hair is permanently outstretched
to heaven.

Those who lack ingenuity
will classify her as *other*.
They will rush in with bulldozers
anxious for renovation.
But she will stand her ground
tag her sacred grounds
with *no trespassing* signs
to keep the demolition crews at bay.
She may not be flawless
but she cannot be convinced
she is fixer upper.
Call her a palace,
handcrafted by royalty.
A temple,
dwelling place for divinity.
A shrine,
living monument of grace.

Beauty Mark

She is most beautiful
when she laughs.
Not the tight-lipped chuckle
she offers in mild amusement.
No, she is stunning
when she surrenders to the tickling
of her soul.
She enchants
when her head falls back
and her chin points skyward.
When a boisterous cackle explodes
from her lips
then tapers off...
and in the seconds thereafter
when her mouth is still agape,
frozen
in silence.
When tears push through closed eyelids
and catch on her lashes,
when she has smiled so wide
so long
that her cheeks pull a muscle.
She is lovely
when she is doubled over
in an involuntary crunch,
hands reaching for her belly
as if to cradle the giggles
and rub the ache away,
when it hurts so good
that she struggles
to utter a word
gasping for snatches of air,
vocal chords strummed so intensely
by hilarity
that they are rendered useless.
She is most beautiful

when she lets her hair down,
embraces the sound
unique to her,
and sways to the loud rhythm
of her laugh.

Preferences

Some people prefer you broken,
Easier to digest.
They lack the patience and precision
To cut through
The layers of strength
Protecting your softness.

Some people prefer you silent,
Easier to tolerate.
They lack the discernment
To separate
The truth of your reality
From the sting of their feelings.

But there will always be people
Who prefer you whole
And vocal,
Even when it is uncomfortable
For them.
Cherish them;
Their acceptance
Will make others' rejection
Less personal.

Midnight

When the clock strikes midnight
On the princess they have made of me.
When the beaded gown and jeweled crown
Lie in a heap
Outside the castle doors.
When my horse-drawn carriage
Becomes disfigured pumpkin
Again.
When I hobble down the palace staircase
Shifting weight
From bare foot to glass slipper.
When my commanding stage voice
Drops to a whisper.
When time's up on dress-up
And Prince Charming
Finds all that is left
Is a woman shivering
In uncovered fear and unspoken insecurity,
Unworthy
Of pedestals.
When all that is regal
Proves an illusion.
When the woman of revolution
Crumples into softness,
They will wonder how this mess
Fooled the world
Into thinking her well put together.
Yet I will not accept
The label of imposter.
I was always real—

Merely concealed
By His grace.
The world saw my essence
Each time it glimpsed
My smile.

I have no fear of a midnight
That strips me of adornment.
The moon's spotlight
Only reveals
The joy of the Lord
As my strength.

little black book

Alternate Universe

what if
after all these years
of calling women crazy and irrational
men are the deranged gender
and women are perfectly normal?

Missed Connection

You were sun
Unyielding fireball
Center of attention
Used to planets jockeying for position
next to you,
entire galaxy revolving around you.

I thought myself
one of those planets.
But time proved
I was moon.
Cool illumination
Patient reflection
Never intended to compete
for your heat
A force
with a gravitational pull of my own
seeking a home
with a star unable to resist.

There is a science
even to romance.
Labored study has shown
your light was too intense
for us to share the same space
without me choosing to fade
into you,
That my intrinsic orbit
deserves credit
for the times I narrowly avoided destruction,
That the balance of my world was dependent
on our recurrent
missed connection.

Ghost Town

Before you walk out her life,
respect her enough to give an explanation.
Grant her permission
to walk the halls of your mind.
The floor boards may creak with tension
as she paces back and forth across
the same issues,
but if you care at all,
answer her questions.
Don't mistake her stalled...
footsteps for miscomprehension,
she just needs time
to take it all in
to breathe
to think
to gather some words that balance
her honest emotions with a semblance
of pride.

You might have to watch her
wipe tears from her eyes
or she may be too stubborn
to let them fall in the first place.
Maybe she will tell you to leave,
perhaps she will beg you to stay.
You may be forced to fidget
under her eyes' glare
or nurse your bruised ego
as she says she never cared
anyway.
Whatever her reaction,
know that she needed it to happen
this way:
face to face
with all facts and feelings laid bare.

Before you walk out her life,
understand that you are not the first man
to make this decision.
Her heart is a ghost town,
deserted by wanderlusts who left her love to die
and call forth its own resurrection
a thousand times.
The inevitable seclusion produced by your departure
will leave plenty of time for self-reflection
and enough confusion
to reach the conclusion that her faults and flaws
are the only explanation.

But if she has the memory
of your voice
interrupting her self-loathing
monologue,
if she can replay
words in her mind until her heart grasps their meaning,
one day,
when the wound is less fresh
and your absence
has become as familiar as once was your presence,
even if she is unable to outrun the regret
of your departure,
she will make peace with it
because of the way in which it was done.
She will find it easier to forgive the transgression
because you walked away without bypassing
an honest conversation.

Porch Light

I left the porch light on.
You could find the way on your own,
but I wanted you to see my heart's greeting
from afar.
Didn't want you fumbling
in the dark
for keys,
didn't dare give you reason to leave
again.

Night after night
I keep the porch light on.
But each time I look out my window
upon an unused welcome mat
lit
by a glimmer of hope,
I wonder if I'll know
when to flip the switch
and let go.

Tomb Raider

I have an unhealthy relationship with the dead.
A tendency to linger at the sides of death beds,
fingertips etching prayers into the blankets.
At funerals, I am both undertaker and deliverer
of impassioned eulogies
filled with guilt and regret.
I am far too comfortable
residing in the shadows of cemeteries,
in dark corners
where sunshine and moonlight do not reach.
I have made a home
of places intended as pit stops
on the way to either heaven or hell.
I have tiptoed through valleys of dry bones,
careful
not to step on anything that might be salvaged.

I have an unhealthy fascination with the dead.
An obsession with dreams, jobs, and relationships
that no longer have a heartbeat—
and it's beginning to wear on me.
My eyes are bloodshot
from sleepless, tear-filled nights spent holding vigil.
My hands are blistered from the death grip I've had on shovels
as I dig graves back up again.
My nails are broken and brittle from prying open coffins.
My back aches from lifting and carrying dead weight,
My heart is weak from the roller coaster of emotions
between expectation of a miracle
and the reality of yet another memorial.
Psychologists would say I have a hard time letting go.
My grieving process
has denial, anger, bargaining, and depression down to a science
but I stall

right at the point of acceptance.
I say
it is the Christian in me,
conditioned by biblical tales in which death was not the end
of the story.
I want to commission prophets
to lay atop my dead loves and breathe them
to life again.
I want Jesus to arrive on scene and say:
Tell me where you have laid them.
I would gladly put my faith in His hand and lead Him
to the tomb
then watch in awe as He calls the dead up out of the grave.
I am Christian—
if I believe in anything, it is resurrection.
And I am Baptist—
every time the doors of the church open
a sermon reminds me
that they hung Jesus high and stretched him wide
on a Friday,
but that early Sunday morning
He rose.
So I have sacrificed things
on the Friday evenings of life,
hoping that someday
they would live again.
But Saturday has become my Groundhog Day,
a merciless time loop of gut-wrenching mourning
that replays
without the dawning of Sunday morning.
I arrive at tombs
to find the stone has not been rolled away.
I am greeted by the stench of once beautiful bodies
now in various states of decay.
This is Old Testament tough love,
God asking:
How long will you mourn what I have rejected?

I have often wondered
how some people could bounce back from goodbyes
ten times more tragic than mine.
Could it be that while I was stalking graves,
their eyes were watching God?
That I enslaved myself to the very thing Jesus died
to conquer?
That as tomb raider,
I knelt before lifeless idols
while the risen Savior
waited for my heart to crown Him king—
He whose relentless love chases me out of the shadows
back into the land of the living.
Perhaps my insistence that God raise the dead
is born of doubt that He will do a new thing.
Maybe I have forgotten
that in the beginning,
God formed oceans, land, and stars out of nothing,
human beings from the dirt of the earth.
Only the faithless have a need to box in
the God of the Universe.
Like creation, resurrection
is unpredictable.
And as Jesus proved in the days between then and his ascension,
resurrection can be unrecognizable:
our dead loves beautifully repackaged
in accordance with God's purpose.

A moment of silence
for the things that were not meant to be,
may they rest in peace.
A moment of thanks
to God who breathes life into the dead and broken pieces of me.
I will trust in His faithfulness,
may I rest in His peace.

Closure

We said our goodbyes in a dream.
The belated farewell
was a beam of light
shone on a part of my heart I presumed fated
to darkness.

It was our most honest conversation to date.
He flinched
at the mention of moments that inflicted
my greatest wounds.
I should have never let that happen,
he said, pained eyes confiding
I was not the only one those occasions bruised—
and I believed him.

I apologized
for my tendency to jump to conclusions,
for my rush to cast him as villain in a script
still to be written.

He admitted
his hasty assumptions and chronic overthinking.
I confessed
my lingering insecurities and habitual doubt.
Finally
Momentarily
We let our guards down.

We avoided
the shedding of tears,
the slinging of insults,
the volleying of blame.

This moment
was everything I had been longing to hear
and all I had been struggling to say,
a glimpse at what could have been
had our two blemished hearts
not gotten in the way.

We said our goodbyes in a dream.
And that was enough for me.
The bitter-sweet farewell
was a sliver of light
leading me from the darkness,
a beacon of hope
beckoning me to forgiveness.

Strays

Whenever he was near
she became a stray at the kennel,
shamelessly staring up at him
with big puppy dog eyes
silently pleading
pick me.

He would stare back a while,
smile as he tussled her hair,
then quietly make his way down the aisle
to the next lonely heart
anxious for a home.

But he always left
empty-handed.
And each time he returned
her eyes commenced
to begging again.

Opposites Attract

Opposites attract
But likeminded people go together.

Whatever intrigue
He has for my complexities,
Compared to his and her similarities,
Is not enough to keep him
From settling
Back into simple familiarity.

Cyber Stunts

funny
we post pictures and musings
for the masses
seeking the attention
of one.

truth is
if he wanted to see your face
        he would set a date.
if he cared to hear your thoughts
        he would call.
whether he chooses to love
whether he dares to change
        will not be determined by quote or meme.

To The Women I Do Not Know

Fancy seeing you here.
Awkward to share the same space as you in real-time
rather than online
where my pride has classified you as phantom woman
who doesn't even matter.
But here, you become human
physical matter and spiritual energy
that cannot be ignored
with the swipe of a finger.
In person
I must face the fact that everything about you is familiar
in a way that should make hellos and conversation flow
with ease.
But I don't know you
and you don't know me.

In fact,
we have never met.
Only crossed paths on the Internet
far too often for my liking.
With one man
serving as our only degree of separation,
the World Wide Web's orchestration
of seemingly random sightings confirms
it is indeed a small world after all
online
where I regularly slip and fall
down rabbit holes,
scroll, hover, and click
until my pride is buried six profiles deep
trying to decode
who you are
to him.

To the women I know of
only through Facebook, Twitter, and Instagram

it was not stalking—
merely surveillance for the case I was building
regarding his relationship potential.
I was judge and jury
and in my courtroom
nothing was circumstantial,
everything admissible.
So when your face and name appeared with his
on my screen,
It was only natural that I investigate—
review poses, captions, comments
and corresponding dates
to determine
whether you had both feet planted firmly in the friend zone
or were running man-to-man in a play
for his heart.
Leaving no stone unturned,
I uncovered things that made me smugly rejoice one day
and silently stew the next.
So I did what any self-respecting woman would do—
no, I didn't cut my losses—
instead I ran down your specs:
employer and alma mater
wardrobe and shoe game
hairstyle and eyebrows
and decided
I was unimpressed.

There had to be some reason
why you were chosen
that couldn't be captured in selfies
and 140 character tweets.
So as Christians tend to do when desperate for answers,
I searched the scriptures
for a text that would suit my purposes.
With my broad brush of condemnation
I wanted to paint you Delilah or Jezebel—
but you fit neither part.

So in my most arrogant and creative Biblical interpretation
I crowned myself Rachel,
authentic beauty who captured his heart at first sight
the one he was going to have to work for.
While you... were Leah,
consolation prize
with whom he'd been tricked into passing the time.

Until today
as I finally see you in real-time.
You are different in person.
More virtue than vixen
more joy than obligation
more sunshine than hurricane.
Perhaps my arrogance was masked insecurity
concealing the fear
that you just might be more Rachel than me.

Some say that social media is the devil.
While it is true that if you resist profiles
they will eventually disappear from your view,
these platforms are only modern-day battlefields
of good and evil.
When we search them with all of our hearts and souls
seeking truth as if it were the gospel
according to Facebook,
all that is revealed is the devil
lurking in us.

So this prodigal daughter is hitting the back button,
retracing my clicks through strange profiles
until I am home again.
And as I come to myself
I will muster all the strength and dignity willed to me
by my Father
to scroll past your face when it appears with his in selfies
and pretend not to see
your clever comments under his statuses.
No matter how curious
I will neither hover nor click.

To the ladies I have disliked without reason
(i.e., because of a man),
my apologies.
Envy got the best of me.
Had we only been two women
without this one degree of separation,
without the unspoken competition,
without my need to cut you down to size
to make myself a better fit for your gifts,
without the pettiness distracting from the business
of charity,
maybe we
could have been
sisters.

How to Hate a Guy in 203 Days

Day 1
No matter how long you've known him
the clock officially starts to run
the day you notice what makes him special.
Whether your knowledge be in-depth or minimal,
start to list the attributes that make him a good catch.
Then get caught up
in the chemistry of your interactions,
the vibe in your conversations.
Make the determination that y'all are a perfect match—
even if *he* has yet to choose *you*.
Just make sure to feel more than you think,
downplay the way he always holds you at arm's length,
making it impossible to get comfortable
in his embrace.

Day 92
Try to keep a straight face
when he tells you he's not sure
what he's looking for
what this is
where this is going.
Tell him that you are not waiting.

Day 98
Dig in your heels and wait.
Vacillate between righteous anger
and reluctant sympathy.
You are furious he senses no danger in coming back too late.
Yet you can also tell he is crushed under the weight
of how badly you want him.
Your desire is suffocating.
He is not wired for this level of intensity,
burdened by the perceived impossibility of your expectations.
You say you want a companion, but he fears you seek salvation.
Watch him back away slowly.

Day 122
Vow not to, but reach hungrily
each time he dangles attention and affection
in front of you.
Feel your heart crack wide open
when he snatches it back.

Day 143
Try to talk yourself out of hoping.
Realize you're not listening.
Go to bed each night thinking *maybe tomorrow.*
Wake up saying *today will be the day.*
Feel your life wasting away
as you give him space to think
give him time to feel ready
give him a chance to catch up—
just don't give him up.
But was he ever really yours?

Day 164
Stare at doors
hoping to see him walk through them.
Stare at a blank phone screen
wishing it would light up with his name.
Prefer pain and longing
to the alternative of feeling nothing.

Day 186
Become a shrunken version of yourself
until you feel like you no longer exist.
Resist the urge to speak your mind.
Walk through life blind to the attention of other men.
Choose instead
repeated rejection.

Day 203
Welcome to crazy!
You are compulsive. anxious. delirious.

Nursing bitterness
like you carried hate for nine months and gave birth to it.
Sit. And seethe,
so angry at this man who you can admit owes you nothing,
yet in whom you have invested so much emotion
under the false notion that it would be returned.
Let it burn.

Day 299
Awake to find
the cloud of dark thoughts and feelings finally lifting.
And after sifting through charred sentiments,
realize it is not him that you hate.
If you're going to hate anything,
let it be your desperation.
Hate the woman you became while waiting to be chosen.
Hate that you held a spot in your heart
in preparation for a reservation he never made.
Hate that you stayed
sitting alone
so long that it is well past closing time.
Hate the time you spent trying to cajole a man
to fill the God-sized holes in your soul.
Hate the way you held out for the miracle of his love,
sacrificing the parts of your heart that no human is worthy of.

Day 303
Set him free—of your wants, demands, and needs.
Set yourself free—of the guilt and the shame,
let it be.
Let the sun rise on another day one.
Let yourself rise
above the stress and regret.
Decide your heart will never again become a nest
for hate,
lest you forget
that at your best
you are love.

Bloodline

All of my foremothers
came to me in a dream.
They wrapped me in arms
that carried more than their fair share
of crop and children.
They cradled my head in bosoms
that nursed babies and men from places
of both plenty and lack.
They rubbed my back with calloused hands
that never lost their feminine touch.
In one voice, they hummed a sweet melody
inviting God into the room,
then handed me a tissue.

Dry your eyes, baby girl.
Wipe those tears from that pretty face.
You got too much of our brilliance
sashaying the halls of your brain
and too much of our determination
lighting up those dark eyes
to let this world intimidate you.

We passed down too much blood
pumping resilience
to that aching heart
for this life to wear you down.
You inherited too much strength
wrapped in unassuming beauty
to let a man break you.

My foremothers knelt with me,
gathering shards of my shattered confidence,
retrieving pieces of my discarded faith,
placing them back in the Potter's hands,
telling me tale after tale
of the times they, too,
began again.

Reasons

a man searching for reasons
not to love you—
looking for flaws and back story
in your every word and movement—
will help you appreciate
One whose kiss
made beauty mark of scars,
The One who could list
every imperfection
yet chose not to run,
The One
who considered it His duty
as much as His pleasure
to pour love
upon the cracked soil of your soul
for no other reason
than the satisfaction
of watching you grow.

Broken Codes

Who says silence
is a condition of staying?
Who determined I must speak in hushed tones
though my heart be screaming?
Who established the line of demarcation
between discretion
and suppression?
Who decided I must censor my story
of scenes that paint you as villain?
Mortal men
are a mix of good and evil.
As you learn to tip the scales toward good,
why must I be quiet when the remnants of evil
stain me?
I too am balancing scales,
learning to be gracious guardian
of your reputation
without suffocating under the weight of truths
unspoken.

As I take slow sips
from a scalding cup of hardship,
trembling hands struggling not to spill tea,
I tell myself
the steaming cup is not burning me,
that my words are not balm
for the next woman's wounds,
that my experiences
are not the seeds of art
in bloom.

Untouched

My body keeps a running tally
of the days it goes without
touch
and responds despondently.
For each week it is denied an embrace
I feel my waist
spreading in silent unease.
Each month it endures without cuddle,
my frame bulges
with unspoken irritability.
Each year that passes without contact
intimate enough to tease
an arch from its stiff back,
my body packs
on the pounds
defiantly.

I am unsure
whether this is a desperate attempt
to increase the possibility
of accidentally brushing up against
random people and things
in order to feel
something,
anything,
if it is
my neglected body's
way of holding
a grudge against me,
or if it is simply a layer
of protection
to keep men at a far enough distance
that they don't detect the desperation
of a woman
chronically untouched.

Second Thoughts

i guess it was for the best
that we packed the scraps
of our pride
and went our separate ways.

but I wonder
if life might be more
joyful
meaningful
gentle
more...
full
had I emptied my ego
and asked you to stay.

Dream

Some days I tell myself
I will be fine
if Great Love never finds me.
I will take
my God
these words
my family
my friends
and call them home.

But once in a while
when I see my dream in the flesh—
a strong arm draped across a delicate shoulder
or a tender cheek pressed against soft bosom—
as I wipe an unexpected tear from my eye
I realize that all those other days
I lied.

Unspoken

Prepare to be eaten alive
by the words you never said.
You thought you could bury them
dug a shallow grave in your heart
and left them for dead.
But their roots run deep
sprout up like weeds
entangled with your roses.
They will slowly wrap themselves
around every beautiful thing
until they have your soul
in a chokehold.
And not until you honor them
with acknowledgment
will they let go.

Oceans

I don't swim much anymore.
Only wade far enough from the shore
to feel the ocean brush up against my hips.
Being fully submerged
produces a head with muffled thoughts
and a tongue weighed down
by words that cannot be spoken.
It feels like submission
to a powerful force whose only loyalty
is to itself.

Yet for him
I would venture into the deep.
Plunge into the dark, wild sea
of his eyes
and occasionally get swept away
in the current of his soul —
if I knew I could count on him
to pull me back up again.

Second Chances

Surely God does not dole out conviction
to have us sit in its mess
indefinitely.
Surely lessons
are followed by opportunity
for application.
Certainly the torture
of indefinite coulda shoulda wouldas
are not written
into His masterful plan.
Inevitably
He will present a second chance.

A Kept Woman

Beneath the shell
of independence
dwells a preference
to be a kept woman.
To have the ability
to place heart, body, and financial well-being
into a man's hands
and trust him to guard them
with his life.
I have secretly and publicly
coveted
women who had the benefit
of strong arms to collapse into
broad shoulders to rest their heads upon
a stable partner to lean on
when life knocked the wind and the will
out of them.

Yet beneath the shell
of independence
dwells a woman
who despite long bouts of singleness
has always been dependent.

A woman
whose heart has never broken beyond repair
whose financial affairs have never known disorder
whose health has been spared serious illness
whose spirit has never been without guidance
A woman who has flirted with insanity
and watched it turn down her advances.
A woman who has been carried
nearly as often as she stood on her own two feet —
even when she could not identify
that which protected
provided
and propped her up.
A woman who
after years of desperately clutching God's hand
finally realized
that even without the presence of a man
she has always been kept.
And for this,
she has always been blessed.

pearly gates

Late Bloomer

Perhaps if I were younger,
greener,
I might be amused
by the sun's regular rounds of peekaboo.
Might beat my feet
in time to the rain's sporadic pitter patter
and slow dance through drought
with the same fervor.
I might giggle
as wind gusts tickled my nostrils with the earth's dust
or as puddles
mixed with soil to gag me with mud pies.
Yet try as she might,
Nature's games are wasted on me.
I am older,
woman, no longer
the tender shoot in the garden.

This is for the late bloomers.
Anyone who has ever
dreaded brunch with your girls because you knew
it meant thumbing through pictures of handsome husbands
and laughing children—
with nothing to share in return.
You who prefer to quietly listen
to the telling of innocuous firsts
rather than at last
face the looming question:
so, what's new with you?
Because you never have an answer
worthy of squeals
or a story and picture reel
to meet the great expectations
of loved ones
or your own fantasies, courtesy
of a Disney-inspired childhood.

Anyone who has wondered
how the same roots that produced
vibrant florals in abundance in every other area of your life
could lie dormant when it comes to romance.

This is for the early bloomers.
Anyone who was a textbook example
of the growth cycle:
advanced through every level
of formal education
with honors,
then watched those seeds sprout into a career
with blossoming salary and position—
yet starved of passion.
Anyone who has ever been pulled up at the root
by your own hands,
then wandered through wasteland and pastures
in search of Eden.
Replanted yourself in a garden
destined for sweet communion with God,
only to have dirt dumped upon your progress,
to drift into slumber starved of water,
and to wake yearning for the sun's elusive kiss.
Anxious to bloom again
and wondering if your relocation
was inspired by the voice of creation
or the hiss of a serpent.

This is for the hybrids.
Those of us unfortunate and blessed
to know the beauty of blossoming
and the agony of being choked by weeds.
The perennials
who have bloomed so often
the world has labeled you low maintenance,
not knowing that each open petal
endured a silent struggle beneath the surface—
through the barrenness of winter,

the budding hope of spring,
the glory of summer's bloom,
and the doom of fall's shedding leaves.

Anyone who mistook resurrection
for a one-time event,
only to die and bloom again and again—
each time as a different species
with a new testimony.
You who were once rose,
breathtaking beauty and prickly thorns that warned
not to come too close.
Then became hydrangea, a saga
of passion-fueled emotion.
Who later bloomed as bleeding heart,
a sob story of love unrequited.
Then as daisy, a narrative
of joy after tragedy.
And finally
a memoir of hope in the form of chrysanthemum.
Each blossom is a poem,
a love letter from God,
who still walks through the garden
in the cool of day,
calling out to the best version of us.
Doling out correction and direction
in the same instant.
Warning that you are not called to meteorology's
attempts at weather prediction,
nor to horticulture's
obsession with the hues and patterns
of every plant within view.
God is still walking through the garden,
pruning and cutting
as a form of nurture,
assuring you and me
that it is our nature
to bloom.

Woman's Work

From the moment
Adam and Eve ate fruit from a forbidden tree
and he told God fault rested with *the woman you gave me*,[17]
the female experience has been ripe with opportunity
for forgiveness.

From the day
a dank dungeon in Cape Coast Castle
became holding pen for African men, women, and children,
the black experience has been crammed with chances
to forgive.

From the second
I put two and two together
to realize that as an African-American woman,
I have been passed down nearly four centuries
of distinct grievances with which to make peace,
I began to resent the burden
of forgiveness.

For time served as *mule of the world*.[18]
For honor denied or deferred
as hidden figure.
For the budgets I've had to reconfigure
based on the zeros missing from my salary.
For use of my body
as object of study and sexual conquest.
For the social experiment
made of my family,
babies ripped from my breast,
mornings in Sunday best
as coffins closed on men and children.
For the struggle to place daughters in wedding gowns
with so many sons on lock down.
For battle scars
obtained for men who gave away my crown.

For features and attitude labeled *ugly* and *angry*
on me
that earned others badges of *sexy* and *confident.*
For the times I've been told to just get over it.
For the apologies I never received
and those offered out of obligation
or for the sake of public perception.
For the ease
with which my forgiveness is expected
and the frequency
with which it is exploited.

I was annoyed
every time I saw a woman take back a disloyal man,
wondered how she could be so soft,
so weak.
I could not understand
how black people didn't sit with their hurt and anger
for a full week
before forgiving Dylann Roof for pumping bullets
into their church members.
I wondered why we always had to be the bigger
person,
questioned whether the black woman's legacy of forgiveness
gave perpetrators the impression
that our wounds
never even pierced skin.

But I learned to forgive
the brave face offered
to offenders and to the world
when I recognized her
as my reflection.
Life became more bearable when I accepted
she and I had the same composition:
too much survivor
to become victim of both the violation
and the need for vindication.

Too much patience
to mistake our declarations of forgiveness
for anything more than the beginning of a process.
Too much faith
to believe ourselves irreparably broken.
Too much beauty
to internalize the ugly we have seen.
Too much truth
to lie down in another's deceit.
Too much laughter bubbling in our bellies
to be drowned out by eternal wailing.
Too much strength and endurance
not to chisel away at a heart made callous.
Too much dignity
to let the world strip us of our best qualities.
Too much hope
to let yesterday hold hostage the joy of today.
Too much light reflecting off our spirits
to ever be overtaken by darkness.
Too much Holy Ghost
to live in a house haunted by another's evil.
Too much Jesus
to refuse to balance a cross of justice and mercy.
Too much God
coaxing us to lay down loads we were not meant to carry.
Too much wisdom
to mistake for burden
what He offered as an invitation
to freedom.

Sabbath

At any given moment
A black woman
Who juggles roles, responsibilities, and emotions
While ducking the bombardment
Of racism and sexism
Is gradually losing her rhythm.
It is undetectable
To the naked eye,
The way her graceful hand movements
Grow slow and methodical,
The occasional stumble
In her fluid steps.

She misses a beat
But recovers quickly.
She misses again,
Resuming less convincingly.
Her hand-eye coordination worsens
And her legs grow wobbly.
She fumbles the items she juggles
And finds herself too heavy
to dodge the world's volleys.
She watches in disbelief
As her roles, responsibilities, and emotions
Fall from her tired hands
In slow motion.
She stoops to the ground,
Scrambling to retrieve them
And reconvene her familiar routine
Before anyone notices.

But in her haste
To return to her feet

She misses an opportunity
To regain composure.
If she would slow her pace
Long enough to breathe,
Let the pieces of her life fall where they may,
Sit cross-legged among the debris
And still herself
Long enough to sit in God's presence,
She would remember
That Strong Black Woman
Is not a name He gave her.
He knows her as Daughter
He calls her Beloved.

Healing Hands

Esteemed higher than
the creativity that piles tresses into tiaras
the vision that parts locs into labyrinths
and the elbow grease that makes kinks stand
        at attention
is the flow of her fingertips
etching tiny circles of relief
upon itchy scalps
teasing out tension
clients didn't know was there
untangling stories
they never expected to share.

More valuable than her artistry
is the comfort her hands weave
into the troubled minds
of those who sit in her chair.

Winter Blues

Every winter feels like the first time
temperatures ever dropped this low,
harsh winds ever whipped across black faces
leaving tear-filled eyes in their wake.

Every winter feels like the first time
night fell with such pitch-black permanence,
that snow relentlessly pounded countryside
leaving brown arms to dig from beneath avalanche
without the warmth of sunshine.

But it is not the first time.
Winter comes often enough to be expected—
yet is infrequent enough that you tend to forget
how bad it can get.

This will not be the last time.
So hunker down, take cover
from the extreme elements.
Pile on extra layers
to protect from exposure
to ungodly climates.
Build fire and friendship
to warm your frigid soul.
If it helps
curse winter as cruel
and other seasons
as conspirators.
If you must
curse the very day you were born.
Whatever you do,
weather the storm.
Even if this is the coldest winter ever
time has always marched forward
to Spring.

Looking for a Miracle

At the top of my faith bucket list,
written in penmanship
as shaky as my conviction,
are three words: see a miracle.
Before life gives one final pull
to the curtain of my eyelids,
I want an up-close and personal view
of the unimaginable.
That which philosophers deem inexplicable.
Something to rival
the stories told to a circle of wide-eyed boys and girls early
on a Sunday morning,
before life and logic bully their faith
into hiding.
A miracle—
like scales falling from the eyes of the blind,
like a whale
spitting the unbroken body of a man onto dry land,
like being thrown into a lion's den
and emerging unscathed,
like being tossed into a fiery furnace
and stepping out with uncharred skin,
like the healing of lame men
for the world's first crip walk,
like waves turned into sidewalks.
I have been asking to see a miracle because a part of me
wonders *what good is a God who doesn't part*
an occasional Red Sea?

But what kind of fool makes a bucket list
of things she's already seen?
How quickly I forget
the people I know who have walked away
from death beds.
That my brother once lay on an operating table
as doctors removed a tumor from inside his head—

without ever picking up a scalpel.
Was it not a miracle
when a friend's doctor said
she had been racing against the clock,
that surely death would have knocked
if she'd taken a minute longer to get to the hospital?
Or when an aunt's doctor
couldn't explain where the cancer had suddenly gone?
I've seen miracles
like people still having a residence
despite months of unpaid rent,
like tires blown to pieces mid-drive
yet no accident,
like random checks
when the bank account is in the negative,
like positive pregnancy tests
for wombs doctors declared desolate,
like holding a newborn baby
that survived the 266 delicate days of gestation
after seeing the desperation
of mothers whose wombs and arms clung
to dying babies in vain—
and no one can explain
why one's outcome was different than the other—
you start to consider our tendency
to classify the extraordinary
as ordinary,
brazenly robbing God of His glory.

So I wonder if the good Lord winced
when I asked what good is a God who no longer parts seas.
Good like my thirsty soul quenched by His living water,
good like all the times Satan led my heart out to the slaughter
and God put me back together again,
good like love at first sight
second chances
and more than three strikes.
Like goodness and mercy

following even the parts of me
that I have tried to leave behind.
Good like life in a world inclined to death.
Every breath becomes a miracle when you realize
empires were constructed by your people's erasure,
systems were created to ensure your failure,
yet you are still here.
That you were born in sin and shaped in iniquity,
Target practice for a spiritual enemy
that put a ransom on your head:
WANTED: Dead or Alive.
But God paid the price
with the miracle of Emanuel.
Divinity descending into humanity,
Leaving a trail
of miracles like breadcrumbs
leading the lost and broken to the cross,
where He, spotless and sinless,
hung among criminals, for us.
Everything has been miraculous
since He took our place
and ascended to the Father
to prepare a place for us.

Now every morning I wake
to His new mercies,
I will pray for wisdom
not to overlook miracles that don't resemble
the ones printed in His holy book,
not to be so blinded by human sophistication
that I fail to see God's orchestration
of every invention, development, and enablement
that we have come to take for granted.
I will pray not that my expectations be managed,
but that my sight-lines be elevated to see
that there are miracles all around.
If I would only seek,
they are sure to be found.

The Unconventional Hero
In loving memory of Motley Younger

Not all heroes wear capes.

For 46 years,
my grandfather draped capes
across the shoulders of boys and girls from around the way,
and fastened them at the napes
of the necks of men who traded in the block for the burbs,
yet still returned
for a Saturday morning shape-up
and a fresh shave
with the precision of a straight blade.
They came to 10th Street and 12th Avenue
expecting community and conversation
stories and playful banter,
but mostly
they came for the transformation.
For when the clippers were laid down,
the chair spun around
and they peered at his handiwork,
they felt like a new woman or man.
And if they locked eyes with their own image
long enough, they noticed
that after taking weekly position
in my grandad's chair, their reflection
was a little grayer, a little wider
than when they first became a regular.
And whether white- or blue-collar,
judge or pro baller,
their style was more polished,
dreams more ambitious,
hearts more generous,
and faith more persistent
because of a standing appointment
with his example and encouragement.

Though they could not articulate when or why,
at some point after his cape first draped their shoulders,
they believed they could fly.

Not all heroes have a standard uniform.
My grandfather liked to switch it up:
tailored suits on Sundays,
with fedora hat or newsboy cap,
scarf and wool coat to match—
perfect fit
for his Cadillac.
Work days
in casual slacks
with a sweater or shirt and tie,
key ring dangling at his side.
Except for vacations,
meant for leisure and sweat suits,
paired with a Giants or Yankees cap.
He was effortlessly fly in any style—
but never too cool
to flash that signature smile.

Not all heroes have theme songs,
fast and furious scores
with complex instrumentation
and lyrical illustrations
of leaping buildings in a single bound.
My grandad
sang of being lost and then found,
his strong tenor
confessing weakness,
boasting dependence
on the Master.
He was content to sing praises
accompanied by organ and drum
or simply to the rhythm
of hands clapping
and feet stomping.

Sometimes heroes
are just members of an old country quartet
whose hymns and prayers rock the soul to its rest.

Some heroes boast love
as their greatest super power.
My grandfather came to the rescue
in times of public crisis and moments of private disaster
armed with a generous heart,
warm hug, and a hand to hold,
understanding that granddaughters
are never too old
for a hero.
He gazed at me
Like the world was lit by my glow,
made sure *I* knew
my value
each time he said I looked like new money.
He smiled through the phone at the sound of my voice,
leaving me with no choice:
I love you, and there's nothing you can do about it.
I recalled those words in his final hour,
knowing that just as my actions bore no weight,
not even death can separate
a girl from her hero's love.
It lives on in my heart and memories,
a reminder that love
is a hero's greatest legacy.

Second Line

This life has not gone according to plan.
This world
has rarely called you friend
while Death
always knows the names
of those you hold dear.
You have learned to bandage broken heart
with the salve of church organs,
their wailing the most honest expression
of your soul's sorrow.
But after the chords have moved you to tears
then lulled you to peace,
remember that your tradition
is more than songs of lamentation.
With God's help
we have always turned mourning into dancing
like second line in the Big Easy.
Ain't nothin' about this walk easy
but we will bop, stroll
twirl and glide
until our misery
becomes memory.

Don't you worry—
Ain't no spectators here,
no one standing by
gawking at your pain.
We are community

With as many differences
as similarities,
but always willing
to encircle your grieving soul,
help it back to its feet,
and parade through these streets
until the rhythm returns to your step,
until the smooth notes of the brass
soothe Death's sting.
We will sing
and dance
until the jubilant trumpet
convinces us we are triumphant,
until the joy is contagious,
pulsing through city blocks
with each pounding of the bass.
We are community,
the answer to the prayer
your spirit uttered
when your mind was far gone.
We are how
you go on.

Beyond

*"I realized I am more than just the widow of [Medgar Evers].
I am my own person." – Myrlie Evers Williams*

The world knew me
through black and white images
of my misery.
The mention of my name conjured visions
of a grief-stricken woman
wearing composure like a second skin.
My darkest hour
was captured
exposed to light
then broadcast to the masses.
They eyed my suffering over their morning coffee,
discussed it while gathered 'round dinner tables,
until they were no longer able to see
past the footage
of my crucifixion
to imagine
my resurrection.

But on my great gettin' up mornin'
I vowed not to be smothered
by a dark veil of mourning;
they would see me
in living color.
I would shock them with electric blues,
currents of my brilliance energizing work left undone.
I would awe them with my untapped talent,
a red fireball of passion shooting across a dull sky.
I would warm them with my golden joy,
rising each morning faithful as the sun.
I would charm them
until their gentility blushed pink
with the observation of a truth undeniable:
beyond the hurt there is still a woman

vivacious and desirable—
soul a vast green meadow
budding with new life,
heart fertile
for love's perennial bloom.

My refusal to be memorialized
in black and white
will be a full-color dream
realized for women blinded
by flashing lights,
paralyzed by pain,
shrinking under the public's watchful eye,
accepting as permanent
a role drawn from a moment
of suffering.
We are more
than the biggest obstacle we have overcome.
Greater than
the sum of our hardships.
We are also
the triumphs and joys yet to come.

We are not meant to hang our identities
on skeletons of the loves we lost,
not destined
to cling to crosses dropped upon us.
Life exists
in the beyond.

All of you
who were present for my misfortune,
grab your cameras, phones, and pens.
Bear witness
as God breathes new life into broken spirit.
Record the moment
and caption me resilient.
Let the joy leap through the picture
with the same intensity
my despair once choked the air
out of a country.
Make sure you get this
because one day I will look back from eternity
at two images side by side
and declare of the aggregate:
This is me
in all my glory.

A Note from Hope

They have tried to kill me.
Tied rope around my neck.
Pumped bullets in my chest.
Injected heroin
Into my veins.
Fed me food laced with poison.
Rigged my home with explosives.
Starved me with policies,
Stuffed me with artificial intelligence
And assistance
That never fulfills.
Choked me with inequalities.
Told me to take this world as is—
Or leave.

You have tried to kill me.
Strangled me with the weeds
Overtaking your mind's garden.
Popped pills to still
My incessant voice.
Slit my wrists
Trying to loosen my grip
On your soul.
Held a gun to my temple,

Told me to surrender
to the terror.

But you cannot kill me.
They cannot kill me.
When you think I have reached my final hour,
When you have made all arrangements—
Chosen a casket and headstone,
Selected songs and flowers—

Before the ink has dried on my obituary,
Before you've had a chance
To bury me,
I'll be born again
In your soul.

Life is my identity,
Resurrection my destiny.
I will always be counted among the living,
And I will never stop asking
You
To join me.

*Blessed be the God and Father of our Lord Jesus Christ, who according to His abundant mercy has begotten us again to a **living hope** through the resurrection of Jesus Christ from the dead. (1 Peter 1:3, NKJV; emphasis added)*

Notes and Citations

1 – James 1:4, *Holy Bible,* New King James Version.
2 – On May 28, 2016, Harambe, a gorilla at the Cincinnati Zoo, was killed to rescue a child who fell into the gorilla exhibit.
3 – Alfred Cleveland, Renaldo Benson, and Marvin Gaye, "What's Going On," 1970.
4 – "Michael Brown Spent Last Weeks Grappling With Problems and Promise." *The New York Times.* August 24, 2014.
5 – "Black and unarmed: One year after Michael Brown's shooting death." *The Washington Post.* August 8, 2015.
6 – Proverbs 22:8, *Holy Bible,* English Standard Version.
7 – John 1:5, *Holy Bible,* New Living Translation.
8 – 2 Corinthians 4:8, *Holy Bible,* New King James Version.
9 – Langston Hughes, "Mother to Son," 1922.
10 – 1 John 3:2, *Holy Bible,* King James Version.
11 – Frederick Douglass, "What to the Slave is the Fourth of July?" July 5, 1852.
12 – Francis Scott Key, *Star Spangled Banner*, 1814.
13 – Emma Lazarus, "The New Colossus," 1883.
14 – Thomas Paine, *American Crisis No. 1*, 1776.
15 – "'A steep price to pay for 20 minutes of action': Dad defends Stanford sex offender." *The Washington Post.* June 6, 2016.
16 – "A Whole Lotta Lil' Kim." *Newsweek.* June 25, 2000.
17 – Genesis 3:12, *Holy Bible.* 18 – Zora Neale Hurston, *Their Eyes Were Watching God*, 1937.

www.ingramcontent.com/pod-product-compliance
Lightning Source LLC
Chambersburg PA
CBHW051838090426
42736CB00011B/1869